D1591914

THE *Wm. McKinley* PRESIDENTIAL LIBRARY & MUSEUM

by Christopher J. Kenney

Copyright © 2005 by The Wm. McKinley Presidential Library & Museum
All rights reserved, including the right to reproduce this work in any form whatsoever without permission in writing from the publisher, except for brief passages in connection with a review. For information, please write:

The Donning Company Publishers
184 Business Park Drive, Suite 206
Virginia Beach, Virginia 23462-6533

Steve Mull, General Manager
Barbara Buchanan, Office Manager
Kathleen Sheridan, Senior Editor
Amanda Guilmain, Graphic Designer
Stephanie Bass, Imaging Artist
Mary Ellen Wheeler, Proofreader
Scott Rule, Director of Marketing
Travis Gallup, Marketing Coordinator
Anne Cordray, Project Research Coordinator

Dennis Walton, Project Director

Library of Congress Cataloging-in-Publication Data

Kenney, Christopher J., 1973–
The Wm. McKinley Presidential Library & Museum / by Christopher J. Kenney.
p. cm.
ISBN 1–57864–310–4 (alk. paper)
1. Wm. McKinley Presidential Library & Museum—Guidebooks. 2. McKinley, William, 1843–1901–Archives. 3. Presidents—United States—Archives. 4. McKinley, William, 1843–1901—Museums—Ohio—Canton. 5. McKinley, William, 1843–1901—Monuments—Ohio—Canton. I. Title: William McKinley Presidential Library and Museum. II. Title.

E660.M149K46 2005
973.8'8'092—dc22
2005010046

Printed in the United States of America by Walsworth Publishing Company

acknowledgments

I would like to thank the board, staff and volunteers of the Wm. McKinley Presidential Library & Museum for their support and encouragement throughout the writing of this book. I would like to especially thank the following people for their assistance in gathering materials and photographs and for their assistance with editing: Kimberly Kenney, Curator; Robin Gill, Science Director; Dave Richards, Planetarium Director; Janet Metzger, Librarian; Cindy Sober, Museum Shoppe Manager; Dick Turner, Volunteer; and Joyce Yut, Director.

WILLIAM McKINLEY

table of contents

chapter one INTRODUCTION

Early members of the Stark County Historical Society look over a model of a canal boat. Pictured left to right are Mrs. Merlin Schneider, Mrs. Martin Schmid, and Mrs. Marie Curry.

On April 9, 1946, a small group of historically and educationally minded friends met in the Memorial Hall at the Canton, Ohio, YMCA. Originally, they planned to organize a Canton Historical Society but soon expanded the idea to cover all of Stark County.

Two months later, on June 5, 1946, the group filed the Articles of Incorporation with the Department of State in

Columbus, and the Stark County Historical Society was born. The trustees held their first meeting on June 17, 1946, in the grand jury room at the Stark County Court House. During that meeting, they decided to make the Canton Public Library headquarters for their new organization.

The Stark County Historical Society would move to other locations throughout the years, finally constructing its own building adjacent to the McKinley National Memorial in 1963. Today it operates as the Wm. McKinley Presidential Library & Museum.

On July 10, 1963, the Stark County Historical Society completed its move from the Cleveland Avenue location to its brand new home. The Hoover-Price Planetarium gave its first public show just three days earlier, and August 4 marked the grand opening for the public. An estimated 6,000 visitors came through the Museum between 1:30 and 9:00 p.m.

Today there is something for everyone at the Museum. The young, and young at heart, enjoy exploring Discover World, the Street of Shops, and the Hoover-Price Planetarium. Those interested in presidential history can visit the McKinley Gallery and conduct research in the Ramsayer Research Library, home to many of President William McKinley's personal and professional documents and photographs.

The Museum has developed tremendously over the last sixty years and continues to expand its programming and audience into the twenty-first century.

This was the home of the Stark County Historical Society, 2677 Cleveland Avenue NW, from April 30, 1959, to July 1, 1963. The house was the gift of Mr. and Mrs. Harley C. Price of North Canton and was also known as the Hoover-Price Memorial.

Current home of the Stark County Historical Society. The building houses the Wm. McKinley Presidential Library & Museum, Discover World, and the Hoover-Price Planetarium. The Museum is located at 800 McKinley Monument Drive NW in Canton, Ohio, adjacent to the McKinley National Memorial.

chapter two HISTORICAL HALL

Early Stark County Home (1805–1836)

In early pioneer days, the majority of American families did not live in proximity to one another, so each farmstead had to be nearly self-sufficient. The ideal place to settle and build a home was near a fresh water source, a river, or spring. Otherwise, the family would have to dig a well.

Most early Ohio settlers lived in small, bare, poorly lit houses. On the frontier, the dwellings were usually constructed of logs and contained only one or two rooms.

Such houses did not have physical partitions, just spaces set aside for sleeping, eating, working, and socializing. Floors, windows, and walls were mostly unadorned. A family might have had a looking glass (mirror) on the wall, but paintings, prints, or engravings were rare.

Food was heavy and coarse. Families in Northern Ohio ate butter, cheese, salted beef and pork, and seasonal vegetables. They made their bread from wheat flour or rye mixed with Indian corn. Current preservation techniques limited the food supply. Few families had regular supplies of fresh meat, so they usually consumed salted meat or went without. They stored root crops such as potatoes, onions, and beets in underground cellars and ate them throughout the winter.

A well-equipped home might have the following:

Top right: Pierced-tin lanterns were used as a light source after the sun went down. The small holes let out light from a candle but kept the wind from blowing out the flame. Pierced-tin lanterns were also used in the barn instead of glass lanterns. If an animal kicked a glass lantern over, it was far more likely to break and start a fire.

Top left: The Pennsylvania Dutch set their bread dough in a dough box, a rectangular bin with slanting sides and a lid that could be used as a kneading board.

Bottom: This long seat has a removable front partition used to keep a baby from rolling onto the floor. The partition can be placed on either side of the bench. The person attending to the child could sit on the end of the bench and do small chores while the baby slept.

Civil War-Era Bedroom (1860–1876)

By the 1860s, inexpensive factory-made replicas of costly handmade furniture allowed middle-class families to maintain a fashionable interior. American mills made fine quality wallpaper, carpets, and textiles at reasonable prices. People now began to "match" furniture in each room rather than using a hodgepodge of different styles.

Bedrooms provided the only genuinely private rooms. Besides allowing people to dress and wash themselves, they served as private sitting rooms for women who lacked separate facilities on the main floor of the home.

People who could afford to do so stuffed bed mattresses and pillows with feathers or possibly hair. The less affluent made do with shredded husks, combinations of cotton and moss, or straw. Everyone stored his or her linen and folded clothes in a chest of drawers, and most families hung their clothes on pegs in wardrobes (hangers were a gadget of the future).

A young lady growing up in the Civil War Era might find comfort in her bedroom with some of the objects on the following page.

This sewing machine ca. 1846, made by Wheeler & Wilson, was carried from Pennsylvania on a covered wagon. The sewing machine brought the wonders of the machine age into the home. Mass-produced clothes in standard sizes became available in the nineteenth century, but most sewing was still done at home on small machines such as this one.

Far left: This hand-carved rosewood bed, produced in the 1860s, is an exact replica of Abraham Lincoln's bed, which is currently on display in the White House.

Top, left: This wreath of human hair was made by Lillie Gratigny Jeffers of Canton. During the middle to late 1800s, hair was commonly woven into decorative wreaths and jewelry designed to memorialize the deceased or honor family and friends. The hair was woven using a series of hanging bobbins and tiny tools that resemble microscopic crochet hooks.

Victorian Sitting Room (1880–1900)

With the onset of the Industrial Revolution, increased prosperity allowed middle-class parents to buy their children what they often lacked themselves as youths.

In the second half of the nineteenth century, nurseries and children's bedrooms, which were new to middle-class homes, held new devices. In this child-centered environment, furnishings included special wallpaper and pictures and child-sized chairs, rockers, tables, and toys. The colonial cradle had been replaced by the metal or wooden crib. The nursery swing, bassinet, and high chair were other new, specialized furniture for child rearing.

A well-appointed early Victorian room might include some of these pieces.

Bottom: In the mid-nineteenth century, society began to define childhood as a distinctly unique phase of human development. Previously, children were seen as "little adults." At this time we begin to see a rise in children's specialty furniture. This high chair (1885) is unique because it also doubles as a stroller.

Top left: The Gibbs Manufacturing Company, established in Canton in 1884, was a leading producer of mechanical toys. In this example, an axle made of wire was designed to produce the motion of the horses' legs as the wheels turned. Many more toys of this type are on display in the Gibbs Manufacturing Company in the Street of Shops.

Top right: In the nineteenth century live performances were the only way people could hear music. But in 1877 Thomas Edison's phonograph changed all that. Music could now be recorded and played in the home. This luxury item reflected American prosperity and increased buying power for more of the population.

Late Victorian Parlor (1880–1910)

The function of parlors, or some sort of "best room," transcended social class, economic status, or geographic location. Parlors, usually off limits to children, served as a stage for special domestic events (marriages, funerals, clergymen's calls, courting, holy days, and holiday celebrations) and as the repository of a family's treasured possessions.

During the late Victorian period, many decorating styles were revived and combined without concern for unity of style. Most furniture pieces were elaborately machine-carved, many with spindle turnings of maple, mahogany, or walnut wood. It was fashionable to create cluttered rooms that included intricate wallpaper motifs with dark colors, heavy velvet draperies, knickknacks, and photographs and paintings in ornate frames.

Entertainment in the parlor provided a diversion from daily life. Family members and guests frequently gathered around parlor organs, pianos, and phonographs to sing hymns and sentimental ballads. The piano became the nineteenth-century status symbol to which a family climbing the social ladder inevitably aspired.

Guests in the late nineteenth century would be impressed with the parlor furnishings pictured here.

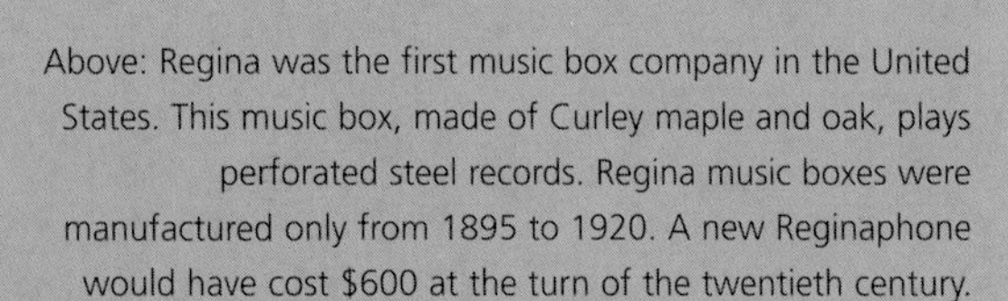

Above: Regina was the first music box company in the United States. This music box, made of Curley maple and oak, plays perforated steel records. Regina music boxes were manufactured only from 1895 to 1920. A new Reginaphone would have cost $600 at the turn of the twentieth century.

Right: This instrument demonstrates the transition from the harpsichord and grand piano to the upright piano as we know it today. It was built by A. DeHuhn Company in New York, and only a few were produced. Henry Beatty of Massillon, Ohio, purchased this piano for $1,000 in 1858. He bought it for his five-year-old son, Harry Tinkler Beatty.

Below: This popular form of entertainment called a Stereoscope was produced by the HC White Company. The viewer fitted a card into wire slots and moved it back and forth to focus the three-dimensional views. Prominent national leaders, beautiful landscapes, humorous scenes, and architectural wonders were popular subjects for picture cards.

chapter three STREET OF SHOPS

Welcome to the Street of Shops!

Prepare to take a step back in time and experience some of Canton's past.

The Worschler Pioneer House

Johann Heinrich Worschler came to Ohio in 1803 at the age of seventy-six after living near Hanover, Pennsylvania. He and his sons followed the scout trail to Steubenville and then on to Stark County. He purchased two tracts of land in Plain Township and built a cabin, church, and grist-mill. Worschler died in 1814 at the age of eighty-seven. He is buried in the cemetery next to the church he built, now called Holy Trinity. The site is at the corner of Middlebranch Road and 55th Street.

The cabin's fireplace not only kept the cabin warm but also served as the cooking center. On the right is a bread oven; on the left, a swing crane for hanging a pot. A well-equipped cabin would also have spider pots, pewter plates, ladles, candle molds, and saltbox such as the ones shown here.

Women's duties were essential for the household to function, and cooking was a major part of their daily routine. When cooking over the hearth, they used heavy iron pots and kettles that sat on the coals or hung on a crane that swung over the fire. The blazing fire itself was hazardous, and women's long skirts had to be carefully protected from the flames. Women were also responsible for making dairy products; grinding sugar, herbs, and coffee; hauling water; and slaughtering chickens.

The Wm. McKinley Presidential Library & Museum carries on the historic craft of open-hearth cooking through classes, demonstrations, and special dinner parties.

Dannemiller Store

The Dannemiller Store is a fully equipped display that takes one back to the mid-1800s. As the town grew, people who settled there were not self-sufficient farm families, so they needed a place to buy things they couldn't make themselves. Stores such as this grew out of the material needs of the community. The townspeople, requiring a place where they could purchase a wide variety of goods, found that the general store not only served their everyday needs but social needs as well. In the rear of the store is a post office that demonstrates the importance and variety of services it provided to the community.

Printing Office

John Saxton moved to Canton in 1815 with a wagon full of printing equipment and intentions of starting a newspaper. On March 30, 1815, he published the first issue of the *Ohio Repository* weekly, one of Ohio's earliest newspapers. He sold subscriptions for $2 a year. A daily since 1878, the newspaper is still in business today.

The focal point of the Saxton Print Shop is the Kaufmann press, named for Peter Kaufmann, who acquired the press in 1832 when he purchased a home on Market Avenue. The American-built common press is registered with the Smithsonian Institution in Washington, D.C. Kaufmann used two rooms on the home's first floor for his printing, producing German-language newsletters. He also printed his own works, including an almanac called the *Western Patriot*. Kaufmann used the press until 1844. It was then stored in the attic until 1957, when the house was razed and the press sold. The Saxton Print Shop also contains a large wooden chest that holds the wooden letters used in letterpress printing.

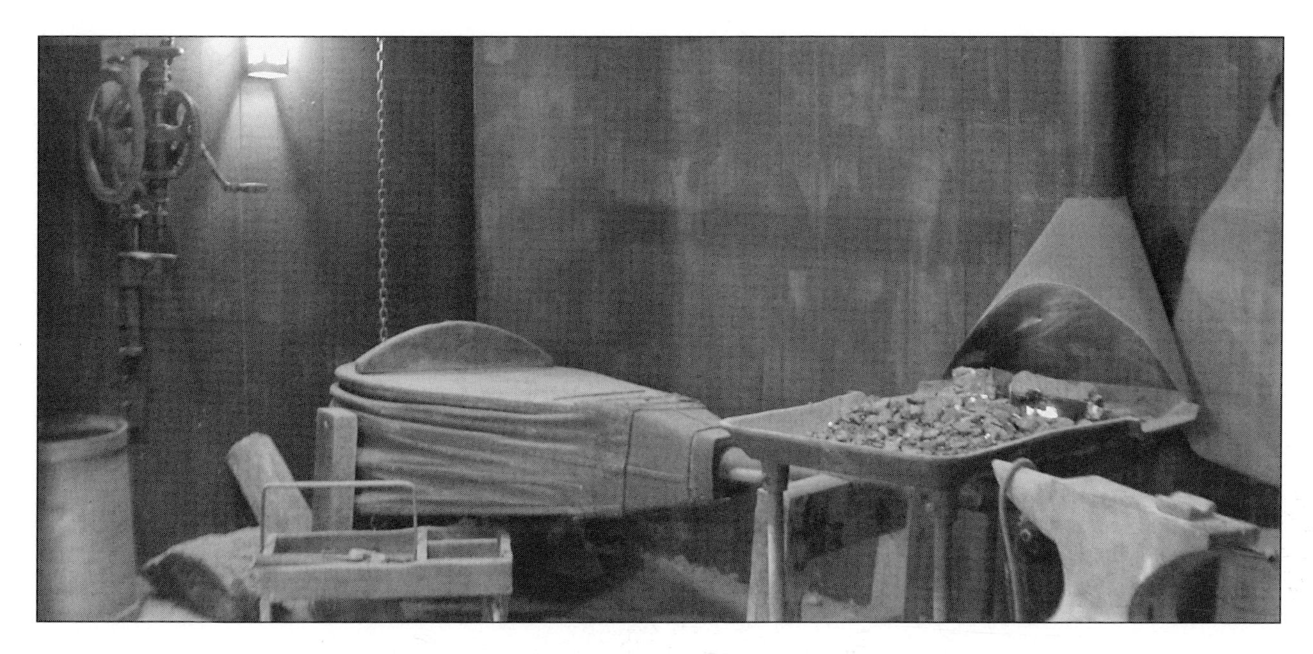

Blacksmith Shop

The blacksmith has been an essential figure in American life since the early settlers landed on our shores at Jamestown in Virginia in 1607. Iron was smelted from native ore as early as 1645, and the colonists needed the blacksmith's skills to produce and repair tools and weapons that they used to clear land, till the soil, and defend against animals and hostile foes. Special efforts were made to recruit ironworkers from England to the colonies. The expanding frontier added to the need for more "artificers" of every kind. Blacksmiths often gained their skills by working as apprentices with more experienced artisans or through trial and error.

The bellows' design is ancient. It consists of lower and upper chambers that are connected by a one-way valve. A few vigorous strokes of the operating pole forces air from the lower chamber into the upper chamber, which is connected to the firebox of the forge. The air blast increases the temperature of the fire greatly and allows the blacksmith to shape the metal more easily.

Eagle Hotel

In the 1860s, railroads zigzagged across the country, and masses of travelers disembarked from the cars seeking bed and board. As a result of this influx of people "passing through," hotels sprang up near every depot. Unlike the earlier small, self-service inns and taverns, the large American hotels of the 1800s emphasized service and comfort. Desk clerks and bellmen waited on guests, and hotels were equipped with water closets, locks on every door, and soap and pitchers in every room. In addition to sleeping accommodations, hotels offered guests daily meals in the dining room. Usually breakfast was over by 8:00 a.m., and the largest meal was served at midday, with a light supper or tea offered in the early evening.

Saloon

By the close of the nineteenth century, hotels and urban saloons in rapidly growing industrial America had nearly replaced early taverns and colonial inns. Canton was no exception. Saloons in particular had become a social center for the neighborhood men, and the establishments were now as numerous as groceries, meat markets, and dry goods stores. In 1898, Canton had 116 different saloons in operation. The typical urban working-class saloon was usually situated on a corner for maximum visibility and was readily recognizable by its swinging shuttered doors. Inside was a counter running nearly the length of the room and a floor covered with sawdust to absorb drips and spills. Beer for 5 cents and whiskey for 10 cents were the staples, but saloons also offered food. A "free lunch" might include frankfurters, clams, egg sandwiches, potatoes, vegetables, cheese, and bread. In addition to being a gathering place where men drank, ate, and played cards, music, and games, saloons provided the city's only public toilet, cashed checks, and loaned money to customers.

Jewelry Store

John Gasser came to the United States in 1923. His watch-making skills earned him a job at the Illinois Watch Company. A short time later, he was recruited by the Dueber-Hampden Watch Works and moved to Canton. He established his own watch and jewelry business in May 1937 in a shop located on 2nd Street NE in Canton. In 1956, John's son, Bob, returned to Canton and formed a partnership with his father: John Gasser and Son, Jewelers. In 1963, the store moved to its present location at 205 3rd Street NW.

Barbershop

The town barber provided many services, including trimming men's hair and whiskers. During the late nineteenth century, men generally wore their hair short and used a side part or, less often, a center part. Mustaches with side whiskers or a beard were popular, although a trend was developing toward clean-shaven faces with mustaches. Etiquette books regarded facial hair as natural, expressive, healthful, dignified, handsome, and virile. In addition, a splash of a little cherry laurel water for after-shave completed the fashionable male's facial grooming routine.

The barbershop also offered facilities to take a bath. By modern standards, most Americans back then were dirty people, but bathing became a more common practice among the middle and upper class during the late 1800s. The benefits of bathing, however, were a source of debate. Some physicians felt that it was detrimental to one's health, and they called bathtubs "zinc coffins." Advocates embraced the practice less as a method of improving personal hygiene than as a medicinal therapy that opened the pores and promoted circulation.

Toy Shop

Children of the eighteenth century had been thought of as miniature adults, but this notion was slowly fading in the late nineteenth century. During the Victorian Era, childhood was "discovered" as a distinct life stage, extending roughly from age two to fourteen for boys and two to twelve for girls. In those days, boys tended to play with toys that were masculine, such as trains, horse and carriages, and baseball gloves. Girls usually played with toys that would help them learn the work their mothers did, such as dolls, sewing kits, and toy cookware. With this modern conception of childhood, the toy industry began to expand.

Photographer's Studio

Photography became a part of American life in the 1840s, when photos were made through a process called daguerreotype. The early photograph was produced on a silver or silver-covered copper plate. The average person did not experiment with photography until the invention of George Eastman's handheld Kodak box camera in the 1880s.

Before the invention of inexpensive and easy-to-use cameras, a photographer's equipment was complicated and cumbersome. It included glass plates, a camera the size of a small trunk, a heavy tripod, and several lenses. Photos taken outdoors had to be developed on the spot. This required the photographer to set up a darkroom tent full of chemicals. The equipment, even for a single day's outing, commonly weighed more than one hundred pounds.

Lawyer's Office

The period in history known as the "Gay Nineties" was probably one of the most colorful and exciting times in the entire history of our country. In those years, there was a certain jubilation in the economic prosperity of the day. The United States was emerging as a world industrial leader, a constant stream of new inventions was making life easier and more productive, and the music reflected the almost gleeful confidence of the day.

Highly educated professionals of all kinds were deeply respected in big and small towns alike, and one of the most highly regarded was the local attorney. People counted on him for everything from traditional legal work, such as wills and real estate dealings, to advice on all kinds of subjects during a visit to the local general store. Very often, the lone attorney in a small town served as a patriarch of sorts, and his opinion was always considered seriously.

The Lawyer's Office in the Street of Shops contains many tools of the trade that were typical of the time. On the left-hand side is a Danner revolving bookcase, which saved space in a small office and made it much easier to locate the necessary reference materials and books. On top of the bookcase is a document riveter, which was used to bind the voluminous contracts that the attorney often had to prepare. The cylinder-top desk in the back of the room worked the same way as a roll-top desk, but the cover is a solid wood cylinder instead of a louvered piece with wooden slats.

This office is named for J. J. Clark, who was elected as the first president of the Stark County Bar Association in 1890 and served until 1909.

Fire Station

For more than sixty years, Canton had only a volunteer, albeit well-drilled, fire department. In 1868, Canton organized its first full-time professional fire department, consisting of two firemen, one engine, and a horse cart. Much has changed since then. Instead of firefighters hitching up horses to the engine, they now have only to jump into their shiny fire truck, and off they go.

This fire engine is the second steamer purchased by the Canton Fire Department and was given the name "Daniel Worley" by the fire department. The Ahrens Company of Cincinnati, Ohio, built it in 1888.

A unique feature of the gas station is the large Gilbert and Baker gas pump. It is classified as a "self-measuring gasoline pump" and has a ten-gallon capacity. The station operator filled the globe to the ten-gallon level each morning, and customers removed as much as they required by setting internal stops via a hand crank. After each use, the attendant restored the gas to the ten-gallon level in the globe.

Gas Station

In the years before the Great Depression, the Union Manufacturing Company produced and distributed throughout the United States an extensive selection of steel prefabricated gas stations. A few can still be found. The gas station in the Street of Shops is a simulation of a Union model and is intended to convey the general appearance and atmosphere of a gas station in the late 1920s and early 1930s. The artifacts in and around the gas station are all authentic examples of items found in filling stations of this era.

These stations sold many other products as well, such as coal oil (kerosene) for lamps, naphtha for cleaning, and various grades and types of oil. Generally there was only one grade of gasoline available, and it was without additives. Octane ratings were not yet developed, and the automobiles of the day would run on almost anything stronger than hair tonic and moonshine.

Timken Newsstand

The Timken Roller Bearing Company erected this newsstand that was located at the main entrance to the plant on Dueber Avenue in Canton. The Philomatheon Society for the Blind supervised the small but thriving business. Although newsstand operators were visually impaired, they sold newspapers, gum, candy, tobacco products, and soft drinks to many customers daily. Visitors can see the Braille labels on the cigar and magazine racks. The newsstand closed on March 3, 1995, after operating for more than fifty years. It is the only part of the Street of Shops that is not a re-creation.

Model Railroad

The model railroad depicts the historical and working relationship of the railroad and the community. Canton was the main distribution yard for the "Pennsy" in Ohio. Trains came from Ashtabula, Buffalo, Pittsburgh, Cleveland, Columbus, Cincinnati, Detroit, and Chicago to be sorted and sent on to their destinations. At one time, there were five yards at Canton. Today only a single yard exists.

Because of its location along railroad lines, Canton's population skyrocketed in the late nineteenth century. Republic Steel, Diebold Safe Company, Hercules Engine Plant, and the Timken Company required huge amounts of raw materials that could be delivered only by rail. Canton's proximity to a major rail line was one of the main reasons businesses moved here.

Schoolhouse

The Seventh Street School is typical of schoolhouses in Stark County around the turn of the twentieth century. In one room, one teacher taught students of many different grade levels.

While the schoolhouse appears old on the outside, the interior is modern and serves as a state-of-the-art classroom for programs for students in grades K-4. During the summer, the schoolhouse is the site for science-based summer camps for middle and high school students.

Davies Pharmacy

By the early twentieth century, pharmacists increasingly relied on chemicals purchased from large companies to make up their prescriptions. However, the art of "compounding" was still essential. Local pharmacies would spread their own plasters, prepare pills and powders of all kinds and make up confections, medicated waters, and perfumes. Pharmacists were also called upon to provide first aid and medicines for such common ailments as burns, frostbite, colic, and poisoning.

The sign outside the dental office is in the shape of a tooth, a popular way of advertising during this era.

Dentist's Office

The dentist's office represents that of Dr. John Weibel, a respected Canton dentist at the turn of the century. When the Stark County Dental Society was organized in 1909, Dr. Weibel served as its first president. This is how his office would have looked that year.

Before oil, gas, and electricity were used to light the dental office, candlelight and sunshine were the only sources of light. Lights designed specifically for dentistry were not developed until the late 1800s. An innovative London dentist suggested that the lamp be attached to the chair, thus relieving the patient from holding the light while the dentist completed his professional work. The first dental light looked like a four-globe chandelier.

It is difficult to imagine dentistry without the high-speed drill. The early drill was a foot-powered device. However, much of the work was done with hand instruments, such as miniature chisels, files, and scrapers.

Most dental specialties were established in the 1920s. Today, a family may make visits to an oral surgeon, orthodontist, periodontist, pedodontist, or endodontist as well as their own family dentist.

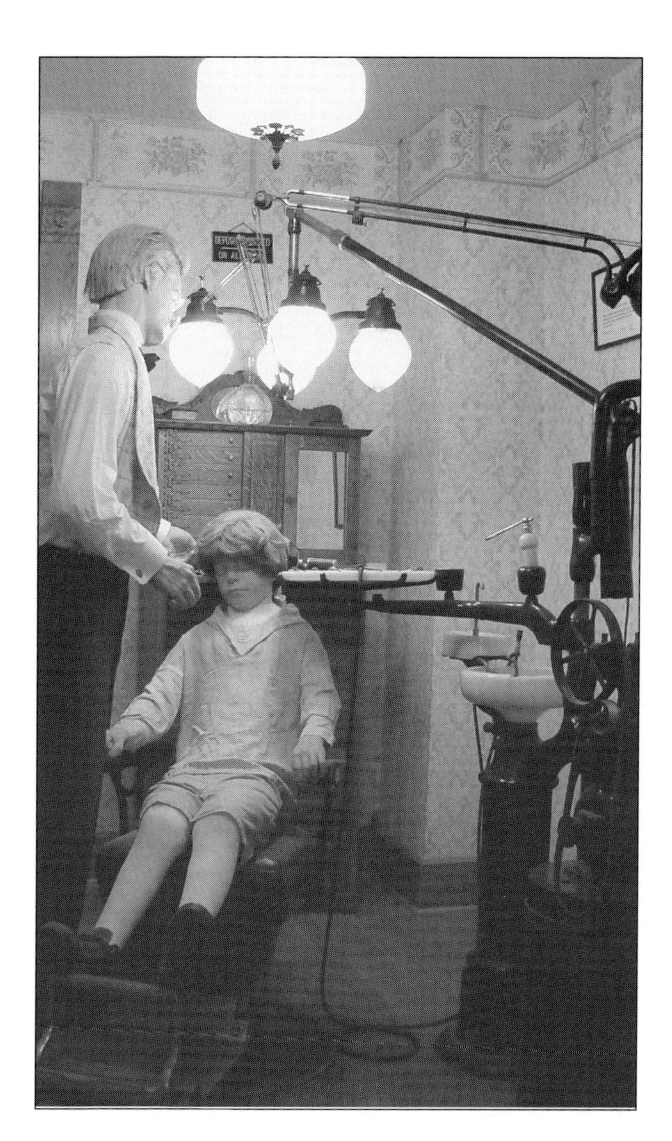

Doctor's Office

This is a typical office of a prominent doctor at the turn of the century. The office is divided into two parts—the waiting room and small examining room. In the waiting room hangs a medical diploma, dated 1898, that belonged to Dr. Baker, who practiced medicine in Louisville, Ohio, at the turn of the century. Prior to this date, certification was not required; new doctors learned by helping experienced ones. Dr. Baker also made some of his own equipment and medicines, a common practice at the time. The examining room contains an antique wooden examining table and medicine clipboard.

Cabinetmaker's Shop

Because wood was the most plentiful raw material available, every early community needed good woodworkers. Cabinetmakers made fine furniture, repaired musical instruments, and built coffins. They were sometimes called joiners because they were experts at fitting pieces of wood together with joints that were held with glue or nails and were invisible to the eye. Planes, drawknives, axes, adzes, and shaving horses were the tools that could often be seen in a woodworker's shop. The most important tool was the lathe, a large wheel that turned a piece of wood so the cabinetmaker could carve it into the desired shape. The legs of cabinets, chairs, tables, and beds were carved on the lathe. When the cabinetmaker completed a piece of furniture, he treated it with finishes such as stains, vegetable dyes, oils, and varnishes.

chapter four THE McKINLEY GALLERY

Born on January 29, 1843, William McKinley was the seventh of nine children belonging to William McKinley Sr. and Nancy Allison McKinley. When he was nine years old, the family moved to Poland, Ohio, for better educational opportunities. Young McKinley attended the Poland Academy, and at the age of seventeen went to Allegheny College in Meadville, Pennsylvania. He stayed only for a short time, however, returning home due to financial difficulties and poor health. In early 1861, after working as a schoolmaster and Sunday school teacher, he took a job as assistant postmaster in Poland.

William McKinley used the artifacts shown on these two pages during his early years in Canton as a lawyer, county prosecutor, and congressman.

Above: The letterpress is an early copying machine. William McKinley used this press in his law office.

Middle: Congressman McKinley used this desk in his home in Canton.

Far left, top: John Danner, one of the first native-born Cantonians, produced these high-quality revolving bookcases. This Danner bookcase was used by William McKinley.

Far left, bottom: Framed citation to William McKinley. This oil canvas illustrates his Civil War record, including his military promotions and the battles he fought. In 1865 he mustered out of the 23rd Ohio Volunteer Infantry as a brevet major.

That same year the Civil War began, and McKinley decided to join the Army. He enlisted in Company E of the 23rd Regiment of the Ohio Volunteer Infantry. After his first battle, he wrote in his diary: "It may be that I will never see the light of another day. Should this be my fate, I fall in a good cause and hope to fall in the arms of my Blessed Redeemer." McKinley need not have worried. He survived his first battle and many others and went on to serve for the duration of the war until being discharged in 1865. Later

At the completion of McKinley's second term as governor, William and Ida leased the home at 723 Market Avenue North, where they had lived for several years. The building became the site of the Front Porch Campaign. The furnishings in the center of the McKinley Gallery represent their home life.

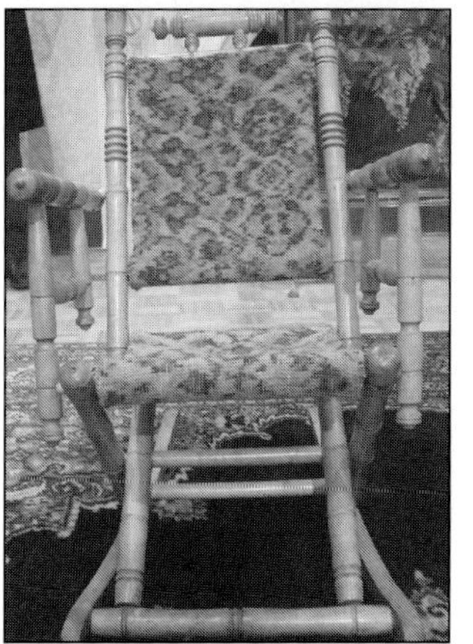

Above: This black Victorian settee, made of horsehair, was used in William McKinley's father's home.

Right: Come to the McKinley Gallery and you will be greeted by figures of William and Ida McKinley. They delight visitors with stories about their time as president and first lady.

Left: This small folding rocking chair with carpet seat belonged to the McKinleys' daughter, Katherine.

that year, McKinley started at the Albany Law School. After two years, he earned his degree and was admitted to the Ohio State Bar. In 1867, he moved to Canton and formed a partnership with Judge George W. Belden.

McKinley was a dashing young attorney and was quickly noticed by Ida Saxton, the belle of Canton. The two courted and were eventually married on January 25, 1871, in the newly constructed First Presbyterian Church. Eleven months later, on December 25, 1871, they welcomed their first daughter, Katherine. Two years later, in 1873, a second daughter, Ida, was born. Sadly, little Ida would only survive to the age of four months. Tragedy struck the family again in 1875 when Katherine died from heart failure.

Despite personal tragedies, William McKinley succeeded professionally. He served as Stark County prosecutor,

Above: This photograph shows only a small part of the hundreds who came from different cities and towns in Illinois to greet Major McKinley personally and shake his hand. The delegations began arriving by train at 2:30 a.m. and kept arriving until noon. Seven hundred came from Springfield, Illinois, and surrounding towns. They wore white silk badges bearing portraits of Lincoln and McKinley and carrying the legend "From the home of Lincoln to the home of McKinley, October 21, 1896." Two special trains carried 410 persons and fifty black horses from Chicago and Northern Illinois. It was the first state to organize a series of delegations to travel to Canton to meet McKinley.

Left: William McKinley won the elections of 1896 and 1900. On the following pages are several presidential artifacts that were used in the White House. The right side of the gallery represents that period of his life.

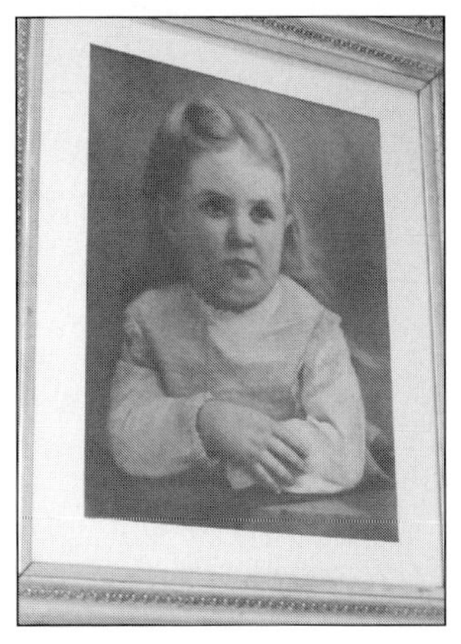

Far left, top: This single Chinese portiere with cord is embroidered yellow satin lined with silk. It was a gift to President McKinley from the Chinese people of San Francisco, California.

Far left, bottom: An enlargement of a painting of Katherine McKinley, daughter of William and Ida McKinley.

Left: F. S. Hastings of San Leandro, California, gave this flag stand to President McKinley. At the time, the United States flag had forty-five stars.

governor of Ohio, and congressman for Ohio, and in 1896 he was elected the twenty-fifth president of the United States. Although the idea of campaigning for the presidency without leaving home was not new, William McKinley, with the help of campaign manager Marcus Hanna, took the “front porch campaign” to a whole new level. Hanna provided the campaign with money, publicity, and organization. By arranging for the party faithful to come by special excursion train to hear McKinley speak, Hanna was able to give him advanced notice of who was coming. This allowed McKinley to custom-tailor his speeches to visitors’ concerns.

People from all over the country arrived at the train station every day. Bands played, and visitors marched and waved flags up Market Avenue to McKinley’s home. For eight weeks, Canton enjoyed this festival-like atmosphere.

Meanwhile, his opponent, William Jennings Bryan, traveled 18,000 miles in three months and spoke to an estimated five million people.

In September 1901, William McKinley attended the Pan-American Exposition in Buffalo, New York. On September 6, he was shaking hands with the public inside the Temple of Music. As visitor after visitor moved past, McKinley's soldiers kept a close watch for anything suspicious. A man shook hands with the president a bit longer than security thought was necessary and attracted their attention. Receiving little notice was the man behind him, Leon Czolgosz, an anarchist and follower of Emma Goldman who saw the president as a threat to the working class and had been stalking him for some time. Czolgosz had one hand wrapped. Noticing the bandage, McKinley reached for the other hand. At that moment, a .32-caliber gun that was concealed in the bandage went off. The president sustained two wounds. The first shot hit him between the second and third ribs. The second struck him in the abdomen, piercing the stomach wall twice. The first bullet was removed, but the second bullet could not be located. Despite the severe wounds, doctors believed his chances for survival were good. However, on Friday, September 13, McKinley took a turn for the worse. His wounds had developed gangrene. On Saturday, September 14, 1901, he passed away.

Above: This unique chair with tapestry seat has carved elephant heads on the arms. The elephant is a symbol for the Republican Party.

Middle: This desk, one of McKinley's White House furnishings, has a leather top and allows two people to work at the same time.

Right: Civic groups from all over the nation produced mourning ribbons to show their grief over the president's death.

chapter five HOOVER-PRICE PLANETARIUM

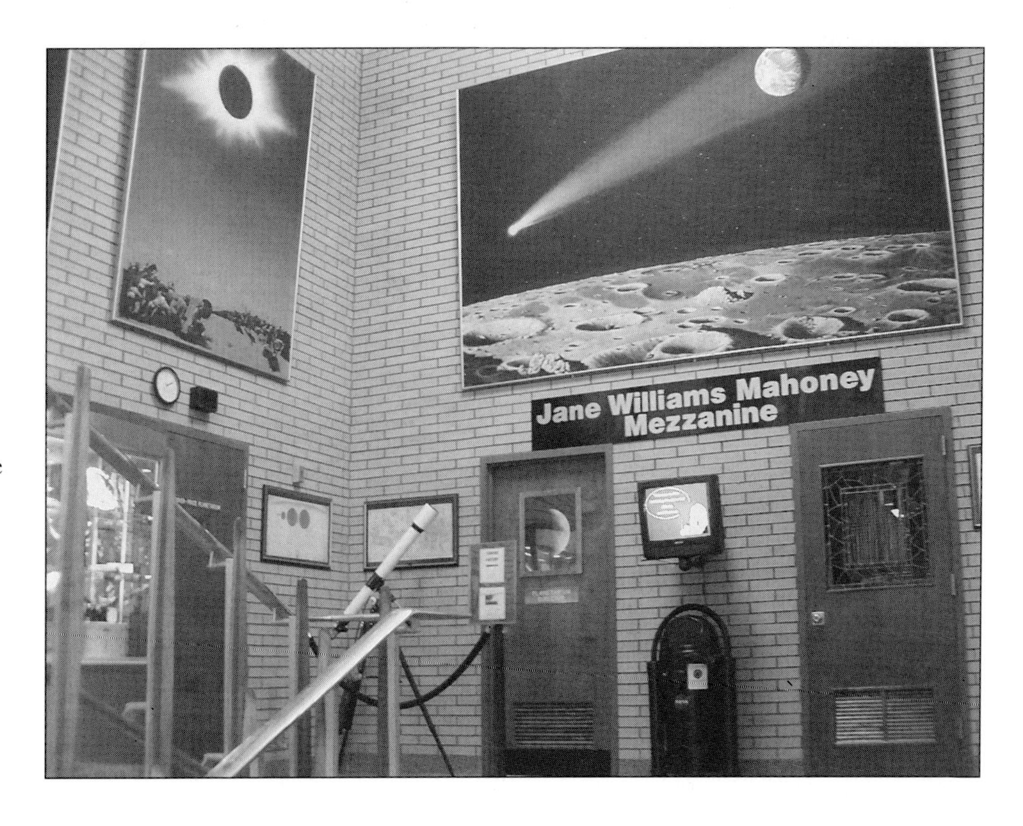

*t*ravel to outer space without ever leaving the ground! That's how you will feel after you experience the Museum's sixty-five-seat Hoover-Price Planetarium. More than sixty projectors show the aurora, meteor shower, an asteroid, panorama of downtown Canton, clouds, snow, phases of the moon, and dozens of constellations.

Installation was completed in 1964, the same year that the current museum building was completed. Since that time, tens of thousands of visitors have viewed our solar system and beyond while in the comfort of the Planetarium. Presentations are offered every weekend, and daily during the summer months.

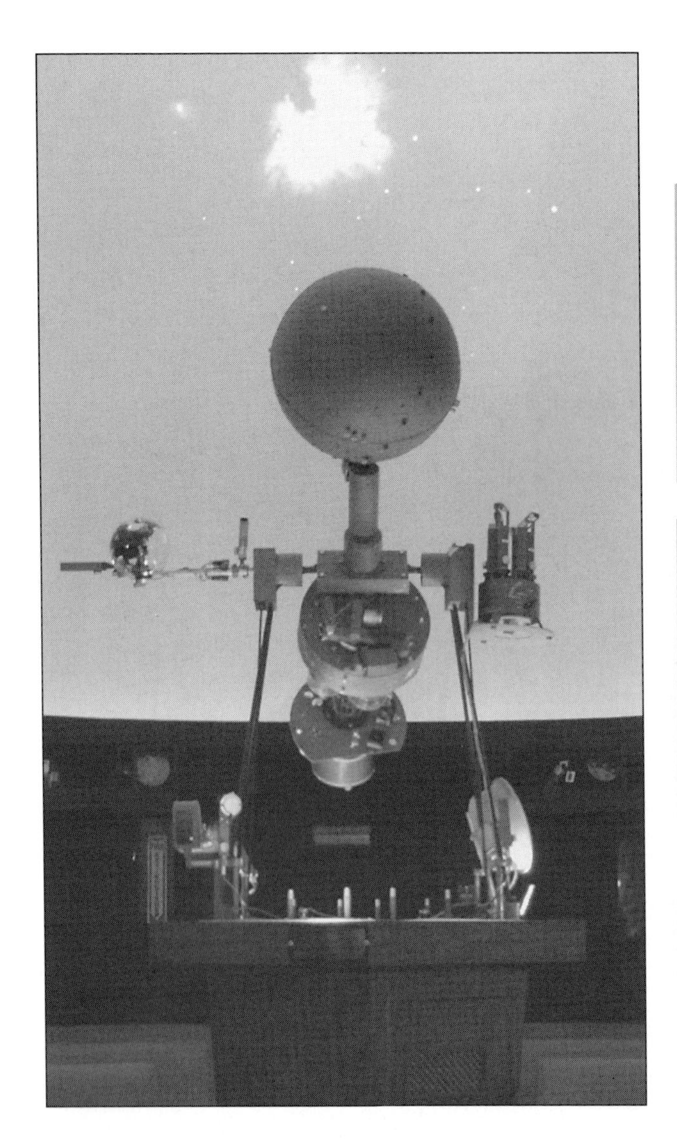

Left: The Planetarium's primary projector is a Spitz A3P that shows thousands of stars in the correct color and brightness. This Spitz is unique because the standard 3,000 stars shown were increased to 5,000 stars through detailed modification.

Below: The operation of the Planetarium is entirely manual. Controlled by 283 switches, sixty different projectors allow the presenter to constantly interact with the audience.

chapter six DISCOVER WORLD

Welcome to Discover World!

This hands-on, interactive science center takes visitors on a scientific journey through the past, present, and future. Travel back to the time of the dinosaur at the Natural History Island. Visit our animal friends at the Ecology Island, and capture your shadow in Space Station Earth.

Alice the Allosaurous welcomes you to the past at the Natural History Island. As you explore the area, you can participate in a simulated fossil dig, revealing evidence of dinosaurs and other life from the Mesozoic and Paleozoic Eras. A focal point of the Natural History Island is an authentic mastodon skeleton whose fossilized remains were discovered in the Canton area during excavation for an apartment building.

Far left: Paleo-Indians called Nobles Pond in Jackson Township home around 11,000 years ago. This replica of a Paleo-Indian hut was re-created from information gathered around Nobles Pond.

Left, top: The DeVille mastodon was unearthed in Stark County in 1970. This mastodon, a young female, lived 12,000 to 40,000 years ago.

Left, bottom: A two-thirds life-size robot of an Allosaurous greets visitors to Discover World with a roar.

Inside Space Station Earth, you will discover hands-on physical science activities for both the young and the young at heart. Learn about the power of air, capture your shadow, experience the power of electricity, and discover the properties of light and magnetism. There is something for everyone in Space Station Earth!

Far left, top: Electricity is sent through the air from the Tesla coil. Demonstrations of the Electric Show are presented on weekends and during special events.

Far left, bottom: The air station demonstrates how air pressure can move objects and produce sound. Visitors can also learn how wind speed is measured.

Left: Catch your shadow at the Shadow Catcher Wall, which is painted with phosphorescent paint. When the light flashes, electrons in the atoms of the paint get excited and jump to another level. When they lose their energy, they produce light for a short time. The only area not affected is where you stand, thus producing the shadow.

The sprawling branches of a white oak tree envelop the Ecology Island. Water trickles down the rocks and feeds the ponds, which are alive with fish and turtles. Within the Ecology Island, visitors can take a closer look at life both on land and in the water, and learn how ecosystems work and why they are so important to the balance of nature. On the following page are just a few of the animals that call the Ecology Island home.

Far right, top: K. C. is an American kestrel, commonly called a sparrow hawk. It is among the smallest and most colorful birds in the hawk family. K. C. came to the Museum in July 1990.

Far right, bottom: Hoodini is an Eastern screech owl and came to the Museum in January 1999. Eastern screech owls are nocturnal and the smallest of the common owls. They cannot move their eyes, so their necks rotate from side to side, allowing them to see things from every angle.

Right: George, top, and Frankie are domestic ferrets and can often be seen taking a walk around Discover World.

chapter seven RAMSAYER RESEARCH LIBRARY

WILLIAM McKINLEY,
CANTON, OHIO.

Dec 11 1896

My darling wife—

I received your message this morning announcing your safe arrival at Chicago which gave me great comfort. I wired you this morning and have no doubt you recd my dispatch. This day has been very much like all the days since the Election—many many visitors, I guess they are done for the day. Everything is going pleasantly here, but you are greatly missed I assure you. I hope you will keep well & come back greatly benefited and have that part of your wardrobe provided which was your special mission. Please give Mary & Sophie & the boys my love & believe me

Your faithful Husband
and always your lover

W McKinley

The Ramsayer Research Library operates within the mission of the Wm. McKinley Presidential Library & Museum. It serves as the county's largest source for archival research. The 25,000-piece collection preserves the photographs, papers, and other two-dimensional artifacts of the history of Stark County and President William McKinley. A large portion of the collection includes papers, manuscripts, photographs, books, correspondence, and audiovisual recordings of the president. There is also a collection of more than 200 written memorials sent to Mrs. McKinley following the president's assassination in 1901.

Reference questions can be answered by phone, letter, or e-mail. Library holdings are available for on-site study. There is no charge to visit the library. However, it is recommended that visitors call ahead to make an appointment.

A letter President McKinley wrote to Ida, his wife.

chapter eight MUSEUM SHOPPE

The Museum Shoppe stocks a large assortment of merchandise chosen to communicate the Museum's mission. From dinosaurs to presidents to stars, visitors will find something unique to remind them of their visit to the Wm. McKinley Presidential Library & Museum.

Books about dinosaurs, nature, and President McKinley are available for all ages. Star and planet locators are great for beginning and experienced astronomers.

Handwoven rugs, made on the antique loom located in the cabin in the Street of Shops, would enhance any home with a bit of history.

chapter nine THE McKINLEY NATIONAL MEMORIAL

The McKinley Monument, a landmark in the city of Canton, is the final resting place for the twenty-fifth president of the United States, William McKinley. Residents of Canton pass by the Monument or walk up and down the 108 steps every day. Traveling on Interstate 77, the Monument towers above the trees. But some may wonder: Why is such a magnificent building in Canton? The answer is quite simple. William McKinley was and is Canton's favorite son. While the president was born in Niles, Ohio, he called Canton home. After his death, it was fitting that the president be laid to rest in the city where his career began, the place where he found his true love and ran for the highest office in the land.

On September 16, 1901, the funeral train left Buffalo, New York, for Washington, D.C. Following services at the U.S. Capitol, the president's body was placed back on the train

WESTLAWN
VAULT

Opposite page: Soldiers guarded the president's body twenty four hours a day at the Werts Receiving Vault in West Lawn Cemetery.

This page: In June 1903 contributions reached $500,000, and the McKinley National Memorial Association invited designs for the proposed memorial. More than sixty designs were submitted, and Harold Van Buren Magonigle of New York City was selected as the winner. Magonigle envisioned a cross-hilted sword with a mausoleum located at the junction of the blade, guard, and hilt. The Long Water and main steps would form the blade of the sword. (The water was drained in the 1950s and re-landscaped.) This design combined the cross of the martyr with the sword of a president who had acted as commander in chief during wartime.

for his final trip to Canton. On September 19, President McKinley's body was interred at the Werts Receiving Vault in Canton's West Lawn Cemetery.

After the services, several of the president's closest advisors, including William R. Day and Ohio Senator Marcus Hanna, met to discuss the location of a proper memorial to serve as a final resting place. McKinley had often visited the site chosen. At one time, he even had suggested that a monument to soldiers and sailors from Stark County be placed there.

On September 26, 1901, the McKinley National Memorial Association was formed, and President Theodore Roosevelt named the original Board of Trustees. The first order of business was to purchase the site, which West Lawn Cemetery owned at the time. By October 10, the Association issued a public appeal for $600,000 in contributions for the construction project. Ohio Governor George K. Nash supported the effort by proclaiming McKinley's birthday in 1902 a special day of observance by the state's schools. Large numbers of schoolchildren contributed to the memorial fund, and the Association was able to purchase the proposed site.

Construction of the memorial began on June 6, 1905, when designer Harold Van Buren Magonigle dug the first shovelful of soil from the site. By November 16, the cornerstone had been laid in an official ceremony attended by Mrs. McKinley and other family members.

Far Left: Workers take a break from the construction process.

Left: Construction under way on the 108 steps leading to the Monument. More than 35,000 cubic yards of soil were added to create four terraces coinciding in height and pitch with the four runs of steps in the main staircase. The steps are fifty feet wide and arranged in four flights of twenty-four steps. Another twelve steps take visitors into the Monument.

The interior dome of the Monument measures fifty feet in diameter and is seventy-seven feet from the floor to the highest point. At the top of the dome is a red, white, and blue skylight. The skylight has forty-five stars in its design, representing the forty-five states in the Union at the time of President McKinley's death. The skylight was part of the original design but for some reason was never installed; there was a clear glass skylight in its place. Using Magonigle's plans and the Canton glass specialists, White Associates, the twelve-foot-diameter skylight was installed during a restoration project in 1976.

By September 1907, the Monument and the twenty-six acres surrounding it were finished. Nine states had contributed material for the memorial. Ohio supplied the concrete, all of the brick, and much of the labor. Massachusetts provided the exterior granite, and Tennessee, the marble walls and pedestal and part of the marble floor. New York, Pennsylvania, Vermont, Wisconsin, Illinois, and Rhode Island also contributed material for the project.

After the dedication, the McKinley National Memorial Association continued to administer the site. Eventually, it became difficult for the Association to maintain the

Right: The citizens of Canton and the McKinley National Memorial Association organized a dedication ceremony held on September 30, 1907. The day started with gray skies, but slowly the clouds parted, and it turned into the perfect day. President Roosevelt and his party were welcomed to Canton at 10:00 by Justice William R. Day and George Cortelyou, secretary of the treasury and Memorial Association member.

Middle: The large double sarcophagi hold a place of honor in the center of the Monument. They were carved from dark green granite from Windsor, Vermont, and sit on a base of black granite quarried in Berlin, Wisconsin.

structure and the grounds. In early 1941, the federal government was approached about taking over the site. With war under way in Europe, it was clear that the United States might become involved, and the government did not want to take on additional financial responsibilities. In 1943, the property was transferred to the Ohio State Archaeological and Historical Society, today known as the Ohio Historical Society. In 1951, on the fiftieth anniversary of McKinley's death, the memorial was rededicated by the state.

The memorial returned to local control in 1973 when the property was transferred to the Stark County Historical Society, owners and operators of the Wm. McKinley Presidential Library & Museum. On September 29, 1992, after five years of restoration work and enhancement of the grounds, the McKinley National Memorial was dedicated yet again. This rededication recognized the partnership undertaken by the federal government and private citizens to honor the memory of President William McKinley.

index

about the author

Christopher Kenney graduated from St. Lawrence University in Canton, New York, with a bachelor's degree in history and music performance. He went on to earn a master of arts degree in history museum studies at the Cooperstown Graduate Program. Chris is truly a Renaissance man with many different interests. He is proficient in open-hearth cooking, has played the piano for almost twenty-five years, has his private pilot's license, and is the proud owner of a 1969 Oldsmobile 4–4–2 convertible. He serves as Ohio History Day coordinator for Region 5, which covers eight counties in northeast Ohio. In 2003 his series of school programs "Ohio & You" was honored with a Commendation Award for History Outreach by the Ohio Association of Historical Societies and Museums. Chris has been the director of education at the Wm. McKinley Presidential Library & Museum in Canton since 2001, where he coordinates the field trips for more than 25,000 children every year.

notes